Rookie
Read-About®
Community

A Day with Mail Carriers

by Jodie Shepherd

Content Consultant

John McDevitt, Postmaster, Ardsley, New York, Post Office

Reading Consultant

Jeanne Clidas, Ph.D.
Reading Specialist

Children's Press®
An Imprint of Scholastic Inc.
New York Toronto London Auckland Sydney
Mexico City New Delhi Hong Kong
Danbury, Connecticut

Library of Congress Cataloging-in-Publication Data
Shepherd, Jodie.
  A day with mail carriers / by Jodie Shepherd.
    p. cm. — (Rookie read-about community)
  Includes index.
  ISBN 978-0-531-28953-2 (library binding) — ISBN 978-0-531-29253-2 (pbk.)
  1. Letter carriers—Juvenile literature. I. Title.
  HE6241.S54 2013
  383'.145—dc23   2012013355

Produced by Spooky Cheetah Press

5 6 7 8 9 10 R 22 21 20 19 18 17 16 15

Table of Contents

uniform

mail

mailbag

4

Meet a Mail Carrier

Look around your neighborhood.
You might see mail carriers hard
at work.

Mail carriers deliver the mail to homes and offices.

From Pencil to Post Office

Want to send a letter to a friend? Put it in an envelope. Then write your friend's name and address on the envelope.

Put a stamp on the envelope. Then drop it into a mailbox. What happens next?

A mail carrier collects all the letters.
He takes them to the post office.

At big post offices, most mail is sorted by machine. The sorted mail is sent to smaller post offices for delivery.

Packages must be sorted, too.

Delivering the Mail

The mail carrier gets ready for the morning route. He loads the mail into a mailbag. Time to go!

The mail carrier delivers mail to houses on one side of the street and then on the other side.

Then the mail carrier moves to a new street.

Many Kinds of Mail

The mail carrier is finished. Now people get to open their mail. It can be a present.

It can be letters, magazines, and cards.

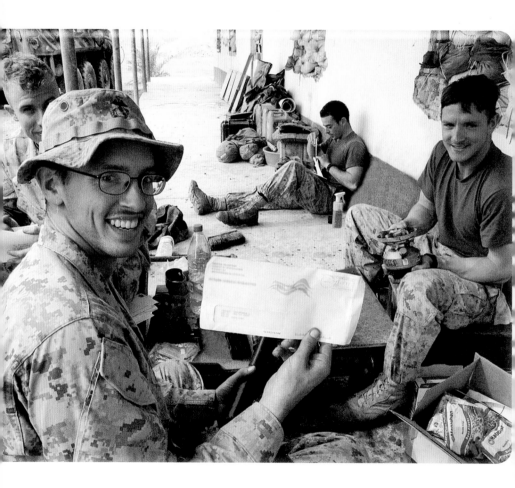

It can be a special delivery that makes someone smile!

Try It! Read page 9 again. Mail a letter to a friend. Do not forget to write your friend's address on the front of the envelope. Put your address at the top left. Attach a stamp and drop your letter into the nearest mailbox.

Be a Community Helper!

- When sending a letter, write the address clearly on the envelope.

- Remember to include the zip code and a return address, too.

- Put the correct stamp on the envelope.

- Never put anything other than mail in a mailbox.

Words You Know

mail carrier

mailbox

package

USA FIRST-CLASS FOREVER

stamp

Index

Facts for Now

Visit this Scholastic Web site for more information on mail carriers:

www.factsfornow.scholastic.com

Enter the keywords **Mail Carriers**

About the Author

Jodie Shepherd, who also writes under the name Leslie Kimmelman, is an award-winning author of dozens of books for children, both fiction and nonfiction. She is also a children's book editor.